wildness rushing in

dee Hobsbawn-Smith

Library and Archives Canada Cataloguing in Publication

Hobsbawn-Smith, dee, author
Wildness rushing in / dee Hobsbawn-Smith.
Poems.
ISBN 978-1-926710-25-9 (pbk.)
I. Title.
PS8615.O23W54 2014 C811'.6 C2013-906110-X

Edited by Barry Dempster.
Designed and typeset by Donald Ward.
Cover Design by Tania Wolk, Go Girafe Go.
Cover Art : "Red Sky at Evening" by Frances Werry, oil on canvas, 48" x 36".
Set in Minion Pro.
Printed and Bound in Canada.

The publishers gratefully acknowledge the assistance of the Saskatchewan Arts Board, The Canada Council for the Arts, and the Cultural Industries Development Fund (Saskatchewan Department of Culture, Youth & Recreation) in the production of this book.

contents

i. little deaths

ii. prodigal

iii. leaving childhood

iv. late bloomer

~ For Mom, who left and came back, too,
and in loving memory of Gran, who stayed. ~

i. little deaths

Descartes' night vision

The Milky Way dissolves
into obscurity,
trail of light-bits scattered

then gone,
a shining river in full flood
the evening before,

an entire galaxy, whitewash
of stars —
vanished.
First being,
then not.

The week Col. Williams confessed

The first snow comes unexpectedly in late October,
soft flakes that soon swathe
the metal braces and rusty frames
of the tools in the farm field.
Our first year here after decades
of Calgary's chinook wind
eating snow and slush in winter-hungry gulps.
But the snow hardens,

and we are walking on ice, black, treacherous,
that will take us down without mercy.
Morning's fog arrives, its ambiguity smoothing
the landscape. Not until the winter sun burns clear
do we see the jagged teeth
of the hay mower.

Insomnia

On sleepless nights, I imagine
your last ride. In the peaceful
turn of years passed,
you shine, lit
by certainty, a boy never a man.

You swing onto your new machine
one April dusk, and the motor
guns like spiraling glass.
Spring moon reflects
on spinning stones
and stars, your
voice fills the sky.
What a night for a ride.

The door closes behind you
like velvet stitching itself to velvet,
sky onto horizon, road onto verge.
Maybe you know, when you hear
the new-woken frogs chorusing
their hallelujahs by the barn,
that the night, that night,
will go on and on,
gravel and tires
whirling, stars wheeling.

There is that moment

When your father's arm stretches
above his head, like an archer reaching
for his quiver, the belt
becomes a snake
in his hands, its scales
of inlaid stones.

Years later, you bite your tongue
and flinch, watching
your long-armed gentle lover
undress.

Taking flight

> "I want to imagine being in my element."
> — Daphne Marlatt

Sun rubs the ashes
from the forehead of the sky,
declares an end
to mourning. On her knees
beside her brother's grave, she absolves
him for his early death,
herself for earthbound limits.

Her element becomes air. She studies
chickadees, their swooping
parabolas, boldly nabbing peanuts
from her palm, pictures
herself as a magpie, the sculpted
tail that knifes the clouds
in a flutter of feathers.

She imagines herself soaring, free
of gravity, liberated
from dailiness — eggs scrambled not fried,
potato soup's breath of wholesome boredom,
greens half-dressed in a lament of vinegar,
feels again that
icy downturn of risk.

The great divide

Driving home from the lake,
the boys and him and me, cool night
dividing us, our separate memories —
hide-and-seek in the reeds, drifting apart
in books, all that remains seasoned with silence.

I am dreaming of a new life, filled with more
sweet crab afloat in wine and butter
when I tilt my head and see
the sky breaking open,
dance of the aurora.

The lights weave themselves into strands —
mallard-green, rose-pink, opal-blue,
amid the watchful stars.
It's almost as if I hear voices of the borealis,
opera of the north, wildly baroque.

Our small boys stir in sleep,
their breath filling the back seat,
while in the front,
a windshield full of stars
weeps for what can't be said.

Cordite

Are you sitting down?
My mother's voice, weighted with stones
handpicked from the south field
where the sand hills rise. On the kitchen stool,
my legs loosen into wilted grass.

Your horse —
his maze of mane, his hobbling
half-gait hoofprints to the hills,
the single set of footsteps returning
in the telltale snow.

Why is such beauty here but to widen our hearts?
In myths, we led our animals
to the temple, blessed their foreheads, knelt with them.
Only humans rose from their knees, blood rivuleting
between stones and hooves.

I hear the aspens sigh,
the scrape of denim
as she shrugs the rifle
into place.
Then the detonated silence,

the cracking fissure between the trees,
his buckled folding hocks
and eyes that now are filled with clouds. And hanging
in the branches, the burning scent of cordite,
metallic taste of grief.

Omens

Morning bending sunlight
into greeting, the bouncing dog,
night-time equanimity spilling out
in squirms and prances.

He escorts me to the barn on his way to waiting fields,
cats gathering, a wave
of greys, a pair of tail-entwined
blacks, can't tell night

from night's shade, the two-tone
tabby hissing at the open door,
skittish young mama,
another bulging belly.

Blithely, I sing,
until I see a tiny fur-covered
mound, a rigid dead
kitten.

I stumble
shaking, to the house.
Our skins so easily perforated, our skulls
ceramic, shattered at a careless
drop. And so few to mourn,
to wrap our fragments
in cotton and silk, to lay us down
with sobs and singing blended in our throats.

Negative space: the revelator

for Cam Patterson

Paint a trio
of birch trees as a tale of unhappy lovers,
their unvarnished ménage.

Along the trees' trunks and arms, shadowed
leaves are cast in greens and greys.
Roots hint at what remains
unsaid, their telling bulge.

Bark, each white pore magnified
and trembling,
each inward-pointing feathered fletch
cut from sunlight, caught,
revealed in its bright mercy.

Villanelle for the mid-summer solstice

Imagine this, the great white horse,
the northern sky in summer,
the gleaming hide of evening's rushing course.

Swathing the night, the starry light-source
drapes us in its coat.
Imagine this, the great white horse.

Air, and light, heaven's best resource,
weave the days we share,
stretching its hide toward evening's rushing course.

The rippling cloth of hours unraveling for the worse,
the loom's stray threads and gaps
unnoticed by the great white horse.

Preserve the legends, coded in deep morse
of light, stars, here, then gone
amid the gleaming hide of evening's rushing source.

Tomorrow's weft and yesterday's warp,
farewell, loss, goodbye.
Imagine this, the great white horse,
and ride regardless into evening's rushing course.

Sailing

in memoriam: Glenn Douglas Smith, 1963—1982

> "Up through the darkness
> While ravening clouds, the burial clouds, in black masses spreading,
> Lower sullen and fast athwart and down the sky,
> Amid a transparent clear belt of ether yet left in the east"
> — Walt Whitman

I almost don't recognize you, wearing a suit
for the second time — at your grad, all hope,
you briefly borrowed formality's blues
and blacks. You have lived in pursuit
of wind on your denim skin, untangling
greasy bicycle chains, their darkness
within your hands like ships' lanyards
dangling, tight cordons of cloud,
drawing you from the day's new-season starkness,
up through the darkness.

You sailed the prairie sky
with kites, tossed upon September's gale
to jig and reel, a teenager's buoyant envoy.
Their flight ordained, you knew they'd fly,
serious as a youth can be about a toy,
and never know its heading.
You held conviction in your hands, your grail,
a born sailor's certainty skirting whirlpool trails,
eddies and riptide currents lightly treading
while ravening clouds, the burial clouds, in black masses spreading.

We lived upon an uneasy tide,
our father's temper an ocean trough
we rose from repeatedly to ride
the struggle up the walls of waves that threatened
to tip us back into the rough
water of disapproval and his angry cry
at a world he did not love and tried to deafen.
But you, you breasted the storms, calm cupped
like grace within your palms, your eyes dry,
lower sullen and fast athwart and down the sky.

Beneath your blue suit and black tie, that calm
has set into stillness, a sailor's final shore.
Not until I am drawn to lay my palm
where your hand clutches kitestrings no longer,
unknotted, fingers clasped upon your chest,
the jacket's fabric, cloud-smooth, uncreased
as your young face, now ageless and at rest,
do I feel your absence
and believe your brief time here was leased
amid a transparent clear belt of ether yet left in the east.

Learning to play snooker at Emerald Lake

Snow hangs in the mountains, camped
in Field's deep fjord, in light
flatter than the valley bottom,
a grey so profound it's nothing but depths.

The highways have closed ranks, Roger's Pass
impossible, the white metal of snow,
the arcing bridge above Golden's gorge
a highwire, steel girders bound with ice.
Only fools would drive that road.

You turn to me, your face like fissured stone,
and I see you know. You pick up
the rulebook and the cue stick,
the cobalt cube of chalk. We call
for brandy, and you break, the crystal
click of white on muted colour.
Their tiny fracture deafens me.

We play as the weather deepens, balls plunging
into ancient leather pockets,
winter racking up the best shots.

Kiss off

Your goodbye
is just another star gone missing,

a shattering turned in on itself.
Scientists who excavate solar systems

will stare in amazement,
say to each other,

their gloved hands cautious on the fragments,
oh, look a broken heart.

Bennett's garage

We stop for gas, pull off the endless highway,
swab our foreheads, hoping for ice cream
to push back the waves of heat radiating from the blacktop.

A beaded curtain rattles on the door, a screen banging loose
against the frame as we cross
the broken sill into a spell-like silence.

The ice cream counter is cool dark,
its blackboard list
grey and smudged.

On the newspapered shelves, we find evidence
of life in 1943: abandoned typewriter ribbon uncoiling
like the snake I saw in the hills, its carbon tongue flickering.

A colour print, Victory Bond girls, faded
cardboard with a thumbtack through their V, framed
by metal license plates, painted numbers cracked.

And a snap of four Air Force boys,
wedge caps askew, their careless years not yet flown by.
They grin from the washboard walls.

Beyond the counter's open window, old man Bennett's
parchment feet are bare, propped up on his desk, his workboots
and socks tangled on the floor, a snore caught in his throat.

We pick out dusty bottles from the cooler, lay our cash
on the counter, and the door slips into hush,
memory's cobwebs closing in

as we emerge into heat, flinch at the roar
of traffic on the road, an SUV's blare of raucous hip hop,
a glossy semi swerving grit past the garage.

To a Jungian

"I have faith in nights."
— Rainer Maria Rilke

I sleep on a velvet blanket
framed by day and night,
the deep river

rippling over smooth-worn stones
while a wild mare
curvets between the canyon walls.

The bed beneath her hooves
carves the way.
She needs no map. I drift

on the tumble and spray of her mane,
held within her mouth's joyful flare
until she surrenders, and swims into the sea.

Aide-mémoire: facing Alzheimer's

Staring at the days to come, she remembers,
then forgets, France. She once
visited the ancient
prison of forgotten women.
Oubliettes, the French kings called them,
throwing whores and mistresses and wives
down their rock-lined gullet.

She can't recall their names,
the lost women's voices
fading, gone with yesterday's tea. *Macarons*
with Marie-Claire on Monday? Or
apéritifs with Jeanne Louise?

Outside the window no mauve
forget-me-nots snug among the paving stones,
no clematis twines along the spiked
bars to frame the view
where her garden was, once
edged with delphiniums,
their stocking-spired arms, their clear
blue stained with white.
The French women, all blue eyed. That,
she remembers, the clear steel
of larkspur.

The forgotten women
scratched their names into the rocks,
the last roses blooming, late, full-blown,
the sea's hungry mouth below.

Leaving Kruskar

for Miloslavka and Milan

Your mother's feet scuff red
dust behind the plough. The cow gone
dry, pulling. Baby asleep,
strapped to her back, whining toddler trails
like floss on her skirt. A woman's legs
are fragile as dogwood branches. No grapes
on the vines. No pear blossoms in this place named for pears,
no fruit this year, the soldiers ravaged it too.
What fruit will she bear next spring?
Her husband is gone,
her brother, taken, spills
his body on the prison cellar floor.

Guards release him. He lurches
as if drunk, so hard to emerge into the light, limbs
flaccid, eyes blind. He has forgotten
the long length of his legs when he runs, lungs bursting,
the pulsing of air within red tunnels. He lives
with your grandmother again, drinks vodka,
                                                            flinches
when the shutters bang.

Your mother plants potatoes in the dead soil.
She is fearful
of guns and men in uniforms,
her neighbours warn her,
Do not cross them. Practice a mild mouthful
of yeses.
She has learned frailty, of trees, vines, bodies,
imagines her brother in that cell,
saying *yes*
            again *yes.*

The old ones caution when she decides
to leave, *expect troubles.*
She wears her infant as a bandolier,
avoids border guards and gated roads,
crosses the river to the frontier, holds
her children's heads above the current.

In your grandmother's basement, her brother stares
at the stained carpet, remembers
the red stones of the prison floor.

Lost

You're drinking coffee, done
with shopping, watching
a young woman, cotton skirt and leather sandals kissing
her naked feet. She rides a tremolo escalator, arms full,
and her turned-back neck with the swan's set
to her throat
          reminds you
of standing on the ferry prow,
your face
        offered to the sky,
gulls and terns crying
around you.

At the ferry's end,
              your bag, gone,
French cotton scarves,
black Italian boots,
your skin untouched, their miles unwalked.

Between that day of loss, and this one,
a lifetime. And somewhere in a miraculous
alt-universe, all the unclaimed,
unmet, unlikely,
            the dishevelled hopes
and promises of a twenty-two year-old girl.

Embolism

As a child she tried on churches
like ladies' hats,

practised scales with the Baptists at noon,
Glo-ow-oo-oo-oo-o-ri-ah,

balancing off-key
along the wobbly high-wire to God.

Angels We Have Heard on High
her imploring soprano

out of time among the pews,
the ordered brown rows of an army.

But Baptists don't dance. She tried
the Methodists,

still meek,
singing at midnight tent revivals.

The preacher's voice was rough granite,
God is polishing your soul.

But she dreamed
of rosebuds and cedar boughs,

twining sunflowers ignited with golden chords,
where wild irises and dogwood brambles

sing free along the river's path.
How will I know God has entered me?

The Methodists were decamped,
no tent pegs left.

No breeze.
Wait
        for the breeze.

            Waiting
was what the breath

was teaching.
But god was jealous,

gave with one hand
behind

his back,
the old bait and switch.

(You never knew
whose voiceless doll

you'd end up.)
I found Jesus, I'm saved

she announced.
Her mother just looked at her,

didn't laugh,
but a ripple rang along the blade of air,

fell, quivering.

            As a grown woman, a hot knife
slides sweetly between her ribs,

its twist a bad joke,
drops her to her knees.

Take this cup of pain, please.
She is breathless,

alone in the garden.
          Dammed like a beaver lodge,
arbutus and weeping willow,

lodge-pole pine and birch,
her left lung failing.

Charred bark and blood,
black rust in her mouth.

          She can't move, pinned
by the knife in her chest.

Time to choose,
the preacher's voice, amplified,

carves the rune-edge of her rib.
The brown and bloody water

of her failing lung
is another flat note.

Dammed, breathless, she hears
the preacher. *No singing,*

you are not
in heaven.

Carapace

A photo of that day reveals you, caught
between sainthood in the order of dweebs
and early eccentricity, turbaned in fuchsia silk,

violet socks that bloom
beneath sage-green leggings.

In your gaudy plumage, you joke about keeping nature
at a distance.
Colour becomes your bodyguard.

When you venture out on the prairie,
your memory conjures
the girl who wore a red wig

every day to school.
It wasn't just her movie-queen composure
that repelled you. The garish hair and clothes hid

a frailty you could not bear. Today,
the valley cleft is edged in white
aspen trunks, their new leaves bright

as knotted shawls among the Quaker grey
of last year's bark.
At their knees, among wild rose spines,

you spot a ruby paintbrush bulb and stalk.
The stark shape startles, you can't remember why,
so you carry the image until it unwraps itself —

the girl in the change room, her crimson pencil
re-etched chemo-stolen eyebrows,
After she lays down her look, a brave calculating dare,

she unwinds her turban, her naked skull reflecting
the unshielded light-bulb glare.

Fear of dying

> "and always death's thin bicycle leaning up
> against the unlucky side of shadows
> the white side that faces outward to eternity."
> — Don Domanski

On his birthday
I try to not let the fear show.
But it does, and he knows.

He moves gently
to assuage what cannot be assuaged —
that he will not again occupy
that bleak Eliot landscape.

I bake another chocolate cake,
gratefully count out candles,
avoid fussing over the fit of his new coat.
He leaves with pockets full,

and laughs before he goes.
A sureness has surfaced in his eyes
that was not visible through that crazed
china-blue glaze beloved of potters.

I watch him walk away.
Plates and glasses loiter on my table,
their shadowed patience in the room each day.

ii. prodigal

At 15

You dig potatoes ferociously. The plants stand no chance
against your fork, flinging soil
over your shoulder with vehemence bordering on hatred.
This apron of a sky, opening and flapping above you.
You look up, but no hawks tear clouds free.
It's your mother's fault you are here. Here,
on this aching-cold day, digging
the vegetables of an aging relative you barely know,
Aunt Tilly, not really an aunt, but they're all your relatives
around here. It's like a garden gone wild, all these second
cousins.
Even think about kissing a boy
and you'd have to check the family tree growing in your
mother's head.
Eating meat and potatoes at mid-day at your grandmother's
yellow table.
Sitting in musty rooms, visiting
great-aunts and grand-uncles who haven't seen you
since you were five, and now are trying to remember
just whose child you are. When you say your name, you try
to sound matter-of-fact about your old west coast life
but it must be a fact recorded somewhere that those who stay
in these prairie towns are fools.
This house, too small in the '40s and '50s when your mother
lived here as a child,
miniscule now for you, her, father, brothers.
Who lives like this?
The potatoes lie blinded on the ground, Aunt Tilly sitting
on a stool beside the garden, talking
to your mother over coffee. You'll never be like
either one of them.

Homesick

The faded light, gone
pale as your grandmother's mauve apron, flung
over her head to shield her from grasshoppers.

The infinite horizon, earth slipping away
beneath your soles, the retreat
of quartz and shale, granite faces withdrawing
into stillness.

The dust of home, toes immersed
in the garden's soil, Gran's arms
full of billowing shirts like cumulus fluttering
around her, tethered
by the clothespins in her hand.

The arcing prairie sky escapes.
Compass tilted
too steeply west, no refuge
among peaks more roof than rock,

clouds tenuous enough to fly through.
Mountains' clipped guardrails.
The knife-edge

grind of routine. It brings you crashing
to your knees.

Compass point

"Small beneath the sky."
— Lorna Crozier

It takes her decades to learn true north. Living
on the edge of the city, she cannot sense
the earth, how it cradles white
onions and red beets. She does not see the owl,
disappearing from tree to dusk to shadow, nor hears
the chickadee's fluted summer tune,
the hawk's wing-whisper on the cross-currents
as it hunts.

Each summer, the wind tells stories,
where it has passed fields
of alfalfa bending, trembling
aspens holding back their secret words, dark places
where moles and badgers tunnel.

The wind insists she listen, before winter
launches another hail of spears. And in her soft
city garden, she hears, and dreams. When she packs
her bags, the compass settles
gently, fixes on true
north. She takes its bearing,
directing the heavens to that point,
sky clearing after years
of storm and angst —
Ready, here, now, strike this spot.

Tracks

Each afternoon we walk the half-mile
to the road, our driveway blown in
by tailing wind-rows
that look like sand,
                                        as if T.E. Lawrence
emptied his robes in passing.
The snow, melted and refrozen, granular
flakes beneath its skin
protected
from the sky that does not end.
                                                    We stop,
inspect the tracks,
today a bird's engraving we do not recognize,
a turkey-toe imprint, too small for a crow.
Last week we saw a moose cow
through the early morning
                                                fog of half awake eyes,
her slow amble a dancer's drawl
across the eastern field.
                                            She left
her tracks behind her, broader than my palm print.
A fawn and doe cut two-toe triangular wedges,
pointing to aspens lit by sunlight, the bark stained pink
by afternoon sky.
                                    We shyly leave our own marks,
snow angels we carve with feathered arms
                                                                and legs, and hope
our prints will still be here tomorrow,
the wingtips slurred by sun and wind.

Returning to the farmhouse

Wait
for your bones to solidify
for your soles to recognize the dust
for your eyes to stop casting out stones
for ghosts to remove their suitcases from your mother's closets
for wild barncats to stop hissing at your back
for winter constellations to shift and realign
for the bed to accept your shape
for the door to swing wider than your hip

Wait   wait
for wheat fields to bend over at your touch
for greying barnboards to assemble into new lines
for the owl to raise her beak and drum down the season
Oh wait

for wind-rows to catch your breathing in their leaves
for sunflowers to tilt their faces to the snow
for black soil to carve itself into rows
for coyotes' song to register in tune
for your throat to open in your own howling

Wait   this place is older
than you can remember   older
than your mother's mother's memory

its patience will outlast yours   Wait for the well to fill
for the morning deer with tender mouths lipping at the dew
Wait for the wind to come again to   upset
wheelbarrows in springtime jest
for alfalfa's green shimmy
for the rusted combine to emerge from the fields

Wait   all comes with time   Walk along the verge
of sand and fescue   past the fading headstone

Late bloomers

A lot under the bridge, darlin',
some things we don't discuss.
You make breakfast, I make
cassoulet. I feed the barncats, you empty
the dishwasher. No deep-fried food,
even though you need fattening up, eat
homemade desserts every night — honey
cake, dark chocolate mousse, rhubarb tart.
Each sweet I make,
another promise between us.

Outside this house spring is melting,
water pooling in the basement.
Never thought I'd be in full spate,
a teenager again, in love at 50.

You take care of me, you tell my sons
right off, settle any outside-edge
grumbling — they know the value
of care. They've lost that white-rimmed stare, hear
my voice, pitched low like a happy rabbit.
Stop looking at me like that.
Might as well tell you
to quit bringing flowers to our room.

Narrowing focus

From our deck, three pairs of eyes —
two binoculars, one telescope, focus
on one bird adrift
on our lake.

Red pupils glaring, face
full of amber tufted feathers, an eared grebe,
not its cousin the horned grebe, not
the coming of death and mayhem, not
the singer of doom, just a grebe on a pond.

We dial and twist, irises widening
and contracting, a sighting
ceremony, letting in
the light, blocking out
those things we cannot bear to witness.

The dead duckling
we buried last week reduced
to a blur on the periphery.

Flood plain

You fear running dry, the ghost dust
of '30s drought,
its desiccation — words might dry right out of you
before you tap your own artesian
water table.

Dredge up last summer,
before you decided to move back,
listening to your mother in the shower,
a child of the dustbowl,
two minutes in and out.

When the shower abruptly
turns into a trickle, your heart
quickens — *the pump the pump* —
and you move quickly,
close the valve, imagining
the pipe running across the yard, from pump-house to house,
the tunnel's seventy-foot plunge to water,
its uncertain flow.

This year the water table is above ground.
You live lakeside, an unexpected generosity —
fifteen acres inundated,
no alfalfa or barley seeded this spring,
the south field drowning four feet deep.

You use your grandfather's rusted
Model A as a gauge,
water now six inches from its roof — it floats
where last year, cattle grazed.

Morning walks take you
two hundred yards east, three hundred west, before you meet
the waves. Inland waves. Who ever thought the wind
would carry them so far from the Pacific,
these crests and whitecaps that chase across
your land?

You rush to write each day, capture the flood
at its peak, green mallards bobbing, heads up down up,
buffleheads and coots, their staccato call a rapid-fire song,
the Mormon tabernacle choir of frogs bellowing
from reeds and floating lengths of wood.

From your second-storey studio, you inhale the funk
of algae bloom, marshiness pungent as duck feet,
ferns and fiddleheads, cattails uncoiling.

Black snail shells crunch beneath your boots, coagulating
in heavy mud, its viscous cling between your toes. You find
egg shells cracked, outgrown, ducklings in shipping lanes
behind their mothers.

The lake brings you gifts — last year's abandoned
tractor tires washed to shore,
a metal fuel tank logjammed on the driveway's
verge. Yesterday you saw a beaver,
its tail cutting a wedge across the gloss,
wondered where he sailed in from,
all these years of small ponds.

Watch the waves, coming plain into view
their lace-edged emerald duckweed surging,
receding with the wind, and you wonder
what the world will bring you next.

The unexpected

Tonight the water is quiet,
sky skimming
the surface with ducks and geese.
Yesterday, there were waves
and wind, pushing
from the southwest as you poled east
to where I waited in the faded yellow grass,
looking for early crocuses.

We envisioned what I had glimpsed as a teenager
living briefly on this farm — lake of sky,
lake of land,
touching like lovers ready to begin again.

We did not expect a flood
nor life beside the water
in the midst of dryland prairie,
with frogs and ducks
singing gondoliers' harmonies as we drift to sleep.

Procrastinator's prayer

We finally say the words hanging there
like icicles: *What if*
the lake isn't gone by winter? Our road,
the panhandle access, submerged
since spring's madcap flood,
an icy autobahn for malingering
birds' passages south?

What if? swims within
the *kuk kuk* of the coots,
the chaotic choking majesty of the frogs,
their black tadpoles listening beneath
the water surface, echoes crazily, w*hat what what?*

How to restore a road
where a lake has taken charge?
A conundrum too large
to consider. Duck the problem,

watch the dabbling
tails of the teals,
the silent purposeful glide
of shy grebes, water changing
blue to slate gray as clouds roll
in. Another downpour, another
inch of tundra ice to navigate
come winter. What comes
comes.

Cretaceous ekphrasis

> "Clever girl."
>
> — game warden Robert Muldoon observing a raptor in *Jurassic Park*

It comes suddenly, the ice. After the flood drowns three generations of implements, machinery abandoned by farmers with more space than sense. The Model A, buried to its chassis, vacant windshield left to appraise the sky. A threshing machine, belts and pulleys silenced. A plough, fitted for draught horses. A combine, its red throat stilled. A '59 Dodge on a ramp, fins tilted skyward, the only vehicle above the rime.

Immobilized, captured until the thaw.

Ice crampons over my boots, I crunch into the void, cautious, test each step. Frozen beneath me, a foot deep, two feet, three, solid as a bad dream. In clear patches, I see the sleeping soil, bubbles like cartoon captions in the ice.

Vertical cracks reveal a geology lesson, and I understand the continents' uprising as I never did, residing beside the Rocky Mountains' jagged teeth. How tectonic plates crash upon each other, forced uprisings and embattled subterranean trenches, if the earth's core should breathe fire again to a Wagnerian score.

I lose one cleat, look backward. Retreat from the auger's long head and tail, in the sunset a brontosaurus, trapped. No swinging club-like T-rex head emerges from the box valleys and tunnels of the threshing machine. No clacking toes of a velocitoraptor track me.

These are dead machines. It's easy to transform them, breathing, hungry, caught somewhere in between. What will they be, when spring comes, and the melt?

Becoming a birdwatcher

We watch waterfowl each morning, peer
short-sighted through the telescope. Each spotting
sends us to the book, a flurry
of pages like feathers — grebe, bufflehead, shoveller, coot.

Through the glass, we see geese build nests,
sail the lake, unknown wings and beaks
defined, sharply focused
illustrations come to life.

I ascend my office stairs, pretending to work,
but their chuckles and laughs call me
to the deck-side stool and lens. A universe
reveals itself, twigs hauled,

striped bills in pursuit of tadpoles, tails
tilting heads down, the effort of takeoff
riffling the lake, the hovering
inverted U of landing.

Their serene lives unhinge
me, and I drink in
verbs effortlessly
as a teal tips up its beak.

iii. leaving childhood

I have been at the lake for ten days

My stays are loosening. I laugh more.
I walk with the imprint of a deer,
its cloven cut in the sand behind me.
My head is blazoned with woodpecker red.

I walk with the imprint of a deer,
my arms are strong from the sails I cast.
My head is blazoned with woodpecker red,
my long sight soars with cranes and vultures.

My arms are strong from the sails I cast.
The fox's yelping bark is in my mouth,
my long sight soars with cranes and vultures.
In my tongue, the language of the secret reeds.

The fox's yelping bark is in my mouth.
I have listened every morning to cattails,
in my tongue the language of the secret reeds,
susurrating, into my sleep, my bones know the paddling lap of water.

I have listened every morning, to cattails,
the loon on the island, the horseflies, even them,
susurrating into my sleep. My bones know the paddling lap of water,
I am losing my fear.

The loon on the island. The horseflies, even them.
My bones are softening and spreading.
I am losing my fear,
tracing snail whorls and arcs with grace.

My bones are softening and spreading,
the lake has caressed my inner shell with its tongue.
Tracing snail whorls and arcs with grace,
my ears are attuned to the owl's radar glide.

The lake has caressed my inner shell, with its tongue
its cloven cut in the sand behind me.
My ears are attuned to the owl's radar glide,
my stays are loosening. I laugh more.

Icarus rediscovered

Two hawks above the valley,
their unrehearsed *paso doble.*

When a feather spirals downward, following
its quill to bottomland,

the creek's slow oxbow,
you see the wind's beginnings in its fletch,

a gust gathering into a current,
the spin of plumage magnified by sunlight.

Molten silver becomes a duet,
hawks' wings a quaver

upon the lace shiver of cloud, a hint
of a dancer's thigh. Listen — *Hey mambo*

mambo Italiano,
those Louis Prima swing-steps,

when the wolf willows sway
your limbs shimmying,

the wind, unchoreographed.
Gather fallen feathers laced

with mare's-tail clouds, weave
an Icarus moment,

lean into your long-plumed
dreams, and fly.

Drawing summer

for Sarah Jane Newman

Holding the pencil like a knife,
her hand cuts graphite lines,

a skeletal tree in black.
Branches burst

from the trunk.
She shades in the implication of roots,

a hint of soil, a skiff of summer on a breeze,
adds an outline of white, sunlit

twigs suggested. At last,
she sketches leaves,

a rapture
of arcing wings, and a cat's paw

of movement
she thought she'd dreamed.

Hejira

Late summer, the sky
is calling like a carnie
as I drive beneath its high blue tent.
Shuswap Lake crowded with houseboats, all
their windows glazed with fire-eater's silver.
Time is a juggler's clock I can't unwind.

Two cases of peaches
in my trunk, fingerprints on each golden cheek,
a farmer's goodbye kiss. As I pass
the ranks of tree trunks tarnished
by forest fire, up the long valley road, I hear
the carousel of vacationers
long before I see you on the marina dock.

Amid raucous celebrations
we climb aboard,
pointing northward toward dusk through the channel,
leaving the circus lights behind, the lake
a melted shadow beneath the moon.
At Anstey Arm, two aspen trees stand sentinel,
the pine forest silent, waiting
behind them. We wake early,
eat peach pie for breakfast
above the pooling water, warm slices
dripping amber, sticky hands we wash in the lake
like paws. A bear
appears from behind the shining trees,
rears on his hind legs, waves us off his ground.

The beach is a sandy palm gesturing
at vanishing rocks and rivulets. We drop anchor,
our bare feet padding down the wooden gangplank,
leave footprints in the smooth shingle.

I see in your face the explorer's dream
of the uncharted, no tracks
beside the stream we follow. In a shallow pond,
four salmon, ghosts,
water brown and green upon translucent ribs,
almost motionless. They know it's not
the unknown we have found, but home.

Rosetta stone

You walk the slope-shouldered labyrinth, unsure
of what you seek, follow the path
within its spiral-bound stones
and hinged corners, dead ends blooming
into unexpected forward motion.

The climb is noticeable. The descent disappears.
Who chose and placed these stones? Gaudy
purples and oranges. Salmon-speckled silver feldspar.
Mottled cream with a crack through its core.
The way was marked by hard
times long before your own.

Your shuffling boots turn
up a blue crayon, and you pause,
trace capital letters on your arm, wax
coats your fingertips like a newborn's vernix,
its cerulean indelible on your skin.

You gather a dandelion,
a fitting gift
in this roundabout world. They say
that the trip is the trip. What if it's true?

The central boulder, four stones away. You could
step over, but implicit rules restrain you.
The back route's hairpin turns fold
and unfold, each graced with last year's grass
nursing itself at the bends.

By now you walk without looking down,
your soles sense the shape. Above, the chickadees play
glass flutes. You speculate where the nests are,
lift your eyes to search.

When you arrive at last at the heart, you give up
the yellow flower. There are no feathers,
but your hand recognizes the heft of a black stone
traced with white lines. Translate it,
and the helix will unwind.

Clockwork

Visiting the hills, study
each footfall twice. Even the groundcover
is alien — cacti that could be needled incisors,
tufted grass like ancient sinews.
Gaze up to unfamiliar sky, gaunt
tree arms without a flutter of leaves.

The knolls look like animals, ready
to emerge from a long sleep,
a crested ridge of spine, a hump
covered with brown coal,
a head in hibernation.

Buried deep in history, the dinosaur
fossils lay undisturbed
until the random turn of a wagon wheel churned
them into view. Now they sleep in the gully,
brown bison and whitetail deer sipping
spring runoff beside clavicles and knees.

At moonrise, the bones gleam
on the pleated grass, lit by abandoned
satellites and dying stars.

Other mothers' sons

He was standing on the median
behind the traffic sign. All I could see
was his red sleeve and the edge
of his stained black Stetson
until I saw the cardboard in his hands.
Change.

I thought of you, and the teenager
I gave a lift to two years ago.
He was sitting on the desert verge
outside of Kamloops, maybe sixteen,
his body almost invisible except for the protruding
angles of his knees and elbows. All he had
was a yellow army surplus pack
and his sign that said *Please.*

Two miles later, I U-turned
across the TransCanada.

Going home to Lethbridge

I took him all the way to Calgary,
thinking in the dark
about growing boys, the highway south.
We went home instead.
Shower while I make supper. You can sleep in there.

Next day at the depot,
I paid his bus fare home.

The immensity of names

for Darl Rowan and Dailyn Carey

Somehow, when his brother chose the second
name, it narrowed and focused
the unnamed.
The baby became more *him*,
more of whom he meant to be.
From the vast
galaxy of potential
brother-ness, one name,
drawn like a slow plume from a sack,
tickling self into being,
as a child's breath
feathers its lungs into opening
the first cry.
You are.
You are.
Be.

Leaving childhood

In your dream, John Wayne struts
off the silver screen, says, *Courage is being scared*
to death, but saddling up anyway.
He whistles his pistols
from holster to hands, too fast
to follow. It makes your breath stutter.

You wake, clutching your sprouting left breast,
find no stains on your bed sheet,
in the blankets, no shell casings,
no bitter scent
of guns.

The next night Dale Evans rides in
on her yellow mare, adds,
A cowgirl faces life head on.
Takes stands. Speaks up.

Buckle on her swagger, saddle
up for another day, pull on last year's
fringed shirt — it's shrunk —
and at breakfast, blush red
as the blood you dreamed
when your mother asks, *Is it time*
to go bra-shopping, honey?

Playground

The year before she stops
trying to out-run the boys, she questions
what instinct slows
                                        her legs,
and does she want
what happens next?

The blond brush-cut boy whose swagger
is stitched into his soul, that
boy, if he
                    should catch her,
then what?

On the field, she kicks the soccer ball
and stops. He slams
into her, knocks
her to the frozen ground, still
                                                            running as she lies there bruised.
Limps to the sidelines
where the other girls congregate, singing,
he likes you.

Back on the field for the second half,
he boots the ball
                                    right to her. Her left foot snakes it,
then she passes it back — he scores.

They grin like brothers.

400 bricks short

for Ignes, Louiza and Maya

I knew when I ordered them
that there were too few. I asked
the clerk, *How far can I make my money go?*
Three-quarters of the way
to carving out a stone bed.

Wearing leather work-gloves
through to skin, I hand-set each brick,
snugging them with blanketing sand.
The girls carry endlessly,
adding to the back yard stacks, their shirts
grey with grit, faces tight. *Lemonade,*
I say, and open the tap. We sit
on our new stone floor, and toast
with frozen tongues and the acid kiss
of lemons the mountain we have made
into a river.

A month later, I see the remaining
stones as they arrive
by barge at night, moonlit.
Invisible hands of silver
lay them in their beds.

Driving the mares

for Jon and Andrea

> "Look at me. You think I don't understand?
> What is the animal
> if not passage out of this life?"
> — Louise Glück

In spring, muddy lanes ripening, drive to where the mares wait to have their dusty coats shone into honey gloss, forelocks disheveled from straw-padded barn, tails parading with each stroke of the curry comb.

Eyes, private waterplaces. Ears, open-hinged pivot-tufts capture the morning's music made by congregating chickadees that fly through the cracking light as the air holds its breath.

The harness upon their withers — Girth. Crupper. Hame. Breeching. Ancient words from countries in love with horses, meanings lost, then found, as lines untangle themselves, align massive ribs, haunches, bellies, string leather reins through blind metal eyes.
Shake the reins and coax them, the plough's long shanks waiting in the sun. Back them into place, quick slow quick slow quick, slide breeching around hips, traces into imaginary lockstep of eight hooves, their legs engage, pistons dinning across the yard.

In the field during high summer, hay tumbles behind the hay mower, falling in languid sheaves behind their heels. Stop for lunch, drop the reins, free the mares to graze, velvet mouths on burgeoning timothy and brome.
Follow them all year, leather reins instead of a rough voice. Their wild-maned fillies running in the grass, mothers and aged aunts gray mares now, their running days done, those years, hay mower rusting in the field.

What are they to me, this massive movement, this certainty on four legs? What they sing, what they slowly dance, what they cleave to, bridle and bit and throat latch, why their willingness? What do they give so freely to me?

Dare

You spend your after-school hours
in the saddle, your horse
your loyal friend,
the schoolgirls in their brief
cotton dresses too fussed
to bother with you and your faded jeans.

You ride the riverbank alone,
admire granite's layered greys and pinks
in the water-polished rocks, the salmon
leaping orange shadows through the noisy torrents,
your hair blowing with the fragrant cedar
boughs and red-headed woodpeckers.

Once, you take the wooden bridge across,
fifteen feet
from creosoted lumber tracks
to rock river bed. No handrails,
its narrow timber tracks
made for logging trucks.

You dare yourself to dismount and check
left and right, the reins a loose
lifeline to your mare. She trusts your sense
and you cross together,
her hoofbeats disappearing down the river valley,
unheard above the water's roar.

Kilns

The kiln, open like an upright canoe,
tips its curved prow skyward. The potters hand-stack its shelves
with unfired bisque, ranks of vases, rows of bowls, planks of plates,
then close it brick by brick, apply mud like a tomb.

Heat and blackness, smoke and carbon, the last breath
of oxygen burns off. What remains —
the unstable pull of carbon monoxide —
invades each clay piece, draws oxygen
from the mud, imprints itself, DNA.
She is falling, the soft tumble into a young mother's half-cooked
egg-like life. Her small
stove has only two winking burners, flames the colour
of yolks, the oven where
egg whites coalesce into soufflé, that trembling
whisper of life and breath.

Carbon edges into her days, warm bed a kiln
that beckons. She fights the urge to sleep into the summer,
her belly set to slow heat. After this child is born,
she will be cool again. *Stranger*
is not a word she uses,
her flesh and its flesh are one.
Mosaic of fingers and toes
the gods bring her to cradle.
A knife-slash of silver severs them.
And she will be she alone again.

The horses call her name

when she's a child,
her hair a mane her mother plaits into ropes.

By fifteen, her calloused hands
are sanded smooth by braided leather reins,
and stirrups turn her knees to hinges.
She's solid as a Shetland,
short-coupled shanks

and a busted Roman nose,
but in the mirror she imagines
a hot-blood's fine-boned face.
Thirty two degrees in Kamloops tomorrow,
and her mother says

No you can't go
to Osoyoos alone with a cowboy
and a trailer full of horses.
At the lake, she strips
the saddle, sheds her jeans, swims with the horses.

While they graze, she turns back to the water
and its silver frame, an Arab mare
gazing, where others see only a pit pony.

iv. late bloomer

Crossing the divide

Beyond the car windows, the highlands rise.
Monotony was all you planned for.

Opening before you, the great mutiny
of the unexpected,

sweep after sweep of valley
climbing to escarpments.

Crank down the windows,
race to the summit,

feel the wind's muscles pull
you up the slope, heart pulsing, fervid

as an athlete's.
At the crest, stop. Enter

the landscape, the momentous rise,
plain and hill-face culminating

in what you can't yet see.
Lean your head into the sky, and open.

You want that vast expanse
within your bones, your skin expanding,

wildness rushing in.

Tsunami

Caught in their tidal wave,
the lovers wash up on a distant island
out of sight and far from view. On a ferry,
when a curious islander
asks where they're from,
he pretends not to know her.
She saw the current's direction then,
                                        couldn't steer away.

His knife-edge letter cuts her
from his life, sets her adrift,
                                a green glass buoy
she wants to shatter.
She navigates daily meals, the shoals
of sleep, her nose pressed
to her broken life,
hoping he will come back.

Anger surfaces, impossible to submerge.
Her pen skims
                  page after page.
She tears sheets and self to shreds, regrets
it all, mails him emptiness. A bargain
struck, her next poem for a glimpse
of his face. Nothing. She sinks, anchor
leaden, tide at low ebb.

The island's shoreline recedes
into the fog. One day she wakes, realizes
she no longer flinches
                            when she hears his name. Her own
net re-woven around her,
day stitched to day with rising sun
and setting words, darkness
come and gone with the running tide.

Foraging

The excitement of the hunt, rooted
in unexpected wonder.

Scuff through leaves
in the woods, stare past

my feet to where diamond rocks
spawn *honshimeji*, boletus, horn of plenty.

Their names soak up the silence
of thousands of chanterelles I trampled

in careless childhood, before I became
a cook, before I saw the richness

of *matsutake*, pine mushrooms, symbiots embedded
beneath Douglas firs and lodgepole pines

like co-dependent lovers.
And morels, wildfire's faithful

follower, their black honeycombs emerging
like charred wood —

beauty after carnage.

Wordless

At a loss for words, I turn to you and say,
let's invent one
for the loveliness in loss,
for green light dancing
above the leaves, the iridescence
of mallards,
for abstinence from desire,
for bereavement when life fades.

I want a word that joins inexplicably
to joy, that celebrates
how I soar
through the air and settle
back to earth untroubled,
how my joints free me for the flight.

I want to meld unfathomable
with elated,
the leap, the run,
the length of thigh in the evening light,
a duck's wings fluttering into sunset.

Looking for the Madonnas, St. Peter's Abbey

I look for you everywhere, Mother, in clouds and trees; only you know if we sprang from ocean foam or a naiad's river bed. To find you hidden in this place of men baffles me, secreted along the corridor walls, in the art studio, the garden. I have counted five Madonnas so far in this monastery, hidden among the faux wall tapestries, Mothers in bas relief, oil, water colour; six if you include the Pietà, in plaster mourning at the foot of the stairs, crazed blind with grief. Why here at all, among this palace of the masculine, the brothers, fathers, abbot, who call themselves sons of god? Some of them fell as satan fell, and washed up on this sheltered beach. Few sisters live here, just four who feed the men. Earnest country cooks, Marthas to another Mary, they accept me as one of them, laugh when I cook, share tips on eggs and baking pans, cheer when my cake stands tall. You are in good company among them, Mother, your face shining in their smiles.

Deadheading spent blooms

Composing a letter to my old lover,
choosing soft vowels, rounded,
no hard edged consonants,
wondering,
what is the protocol?
Be happy for me, I am joyful?
Be sad for us, we are ended?

We never had a summer.
We went from first blossom to sere.
And now, I am writing letters,
saying *love* and *forever* and *hope*,
those untended blooms we couldn't grow.
I want your blessing, be glad for me.

To begin

after "Becoming a writer" by Dave Margoshes

For years, I thought writing
a poem no small affair, but no big
deal either.

I overlooked so much,
gazed past the curve of the coast,
ignored the countless
words like shells on a dozen shores,
too many to choose
among, surely, and how to prize
a turquoise noun
above an amber scalloped verb?

I under-estimated the halting
pause of a line
at the tip of a wave
as it waits
to hear itself, and fall.

The end of the drought

for Phil Hall

Quaking aspens along the river
open their gazelle throats to the sky,

as if emerald leaf-coins sheered
with silver drops can buy heaven,

as if young limbs assure
endurance. As if they have

never harboured naiads behind their trunks,
never watched them step forth,

dainty-footed,
antlered fingers branched

around nightshade-deadly
knives with horn handles.

Aspens drink with abandon, they know
rain comes only now and then,

to those rooted deep, those wise enough
to open themselves to the sky.

The meaning of red

after Zhang Yimou's "Ju Dou"

Two hours. The cinematic wheel's
impartial turn, Gong Li again upon the karmic arc, Techni-
color

canvas. Her sullen face,
husband, lover, son — stained by anger,

one generation to the next
suffused with scarlet.

Afternoon is pallid
when I emerge.

From you, master director, I adopt art,
abandon impotence, open

the tins with a screwdriver, gaze
at pools of carmine, crimson, cardinal. In past

years, I dabbled, a paintbrush clenched
in one hand, crept along the window ledge.

Today, I grasp each tin two-handed, hurl everything
against the sky, watch it flow and sail,

setting into the wind,
no maybe, no failing.

Growing

> "... and laid its shining weapons down."
> — Karen Solie

She tends the roses,
clips the withered leaves,
deadheads finished blooms, cuts
blossoms for the table facing east.

She chooses where to place her spade, unearths
young potatoes in their bed, the season
in their new eyes. She welcomes sunlight,

the same way the soil
beneath her boots accepts —
more rain last year, a drought in spring.

She is finally able to say grace
over the bones of love.
She has burned old letters that have seared
her with their heat.

Today she totes the ashes
to the garden. There is a use for everything.
She turns the layers, hopes
for growth, and prays for rain.

The real meaning of pink

how do you feel about cherries? you can't leave
them alone, spit the pits
as far as next week, your mouth stained with life —
so what took you so long to arrive?
it isn't anything that takes a degree,
you just let go

the universe's liberal arts program in colour
a hand-painted sign
that says fuck the world
and i like what i like — yell
yourself hoarse on the windward
side of flash, dot-matrix morse code
advertising organ donor quilts as *aides-mémoires*

think juicy
jouissance, your mouth
too shy to wrap itself around the syllables of desire
orchids opening, berries succumbing
beneath your tongue, juicy cherries,
that tiger chrysanthemum won't bite

surrender to wearing jeans and boots
with silk, that cowboy hat
you've been hoarding, why not
take it to the beach and offer it
a cyclamen of its own, butterflies
with leopards' wings, witnessing their weft
of incandescent silk, a drifting scarf

while you're airborne, watch for angels' feathers
the colour of carnivals, tour the circus, offer
to paint the zebras, slather pigment outside
the lines, not suitable for the shy
startling, what you cannot contain
inside a polka dot tote

Bad bones

My father's bad ankle, broken
in a bike race at 17,
his left-legged limp a slow stutter
leaning on the off
syllables. My mother's knees, gone
to the recycling plant, skeleton
of wire and joints of titanium, strung
to screws and bits of bone.

My lover's ankles,
their bend and sway, curved
shanks that will not survive a shipwreck,
carry him through the storm, his gait marking
him as a sailor.

I wonder what limping masks and reveals.
A shortening of psychic tendons,
a calcification of dreams?
I worry it might be ambition
bounding ahead, careless of skeletons
and skin, defeated double hobbling home.
I pray,
take minerals, lift weights,
build a sturdy frame, prepare
to make my leap.

Pears

For three days I resist
the yellow pears, restrain my hands
from touching their perfect arcs.

Their bell-curves in the bowl
remind me of seals,
porpoises, otters, the unselfconscious

sinuous grace of childhood,
my sons' slides and climbing trees.
How did I become a mother?

Bells tolling, years I don't feel
old enough to acknowledge.
Gone, my otter hips,

grown into my own pear curves.

Contemplating breast surgery

for Judith

A breast is a simple thing
to cooks and surgeons, the recipe's
clear print —
one breast, boneless —
drooping soft from the breastbone,
no muscles or tendons or ribcage to protect it
from the cull and call of hunger,
and eager cutting hands.
One breast or half?
How much is enough?

French cooks, tired of wrestling with such questions,
name pairs or parts or singles
together in submission beneath the knife:
magret.

But surgeons and chefs
forget curve and touch and tenderness. In the flesh,
I prefer uncut
feminine names, round with open
vowels and sweet sibilant consonants,

name them in private rooms.
Meet my breasts:
Francesca. Consuela.

Waiting for the loons

This confluence of lives, unpacking
in an old cabin, sharing a new shore.
We ignore each gap and potential fissure, find rests
for your papers, my bathrobe,
both toothbrushes.

From the lake, the singing island
calls. I hear the wind in the rushes,
but not the voices I hope
to hear, their violins in a haunting
minor key, wildness in every phrase
and bow-stroke.

Your hair is spread across our pillow.
Mine is tangled
among the reeds
where the gypsy music plays.

Communication

One minute I execute the perfect
dive through the flames
of a burning hoop. The next, I'm jaw-to-jaw
with a tiger, orange smoke and charcoal
looking for an excuse to ignite.

A swan of a long walk, peaceful dust,
tracks to the veldt's next town, breathing
the giraffe's tall air. Along the way, kneel
close to the riverbank's mud,
translate the hieroglyphics embedded there —
hippos' fat footprints, the scrape and sing of a flamingo's wings.

A mother knows. Practicality is her favourite button-
down sweater, how her hands make sense
of the thread of things, the pulls of warp and weft,
the many pedals of the loom.

She might be magpie, drawn to shot-gold thread,
she looks for silk, not tweed. But she knows
what's best, to shear and card and spin.
Dye it, weave it, unfold a tartan for her boys.
Next day she'll make an entire bolt from scratch.

You'd blossom with my silver rope,
transformation spun from my horn
into your empty spaces. I fill you

with imaginings — how a girl breathes —
a little glitter, faery dust
like the shimmer of my hooves — beauty
you don't know yet. Your kindness could kill you.

You're the spell-caster in a cloak of stars,
weaving legends with birch bark and aspen shadows,
part Diana's daughter, part Irish *sidhe,*
who arrives by standing still.

Beloved at 51

for Dave

She wasn't born a beauty, her cheeks planed
and plunging, nose arched
like a Roman-bred mare's.

Life has left scars, broken
bones and faith, lost friends and lovers,
chasms and contradictions.

She learns
to dine alone, her eyes shielded
by her forelock.

Peace becomes her,
the book, the meal, the day,
wearing solitude like a prayer shawl.

When they met, late lovers, they celebrated a new
year, even as she counted on her fingers
those already flown.

Beautiful, he tells her,
and in a certain light,
she believes him.

Phoenix

We hitch heavy horses to our wagons,
haul the rubble of our broken
homes into the courtyard,
armoires emptied
of meaning, double
beds we cannot share,
and strike a match.

We start again,
hang doors, build lintels,
breathe hope
into every dovetailed joint.

We pray,
and cross the threshold.

Poem posted on the ship's starboard door

Pull.
Magnetic ions rattle loose in his blood,
his radar locked when he crosses
her path, his particles charged
with aches he cannot identify or locate, maverick
monkey-stars set adrift from their orbit.

Watch your step.
When they collide,
his eyes slide down
her cotton skirt, flesh exposed to the breeze,
lifts above her knees as she ascend the stairs.
He imagines she is climbing him.

Mind your head.
There's nothing intelligent about falling
in love. Depth charges are always unexpected.
He hears no time clock, no ticking
of the watch. Star-shot possibilities reverberate
when she speaks, familiar
phrases blindsided, disrupted.

Deck slippery when wet.
Her towel pools beneath her hips as she reclines
on the chaise. His gaze slides
around the southern curve
his hand has mapped in dreams.

Beware of strong winds.
He imagines kissing her,
the gale, the lull. Unseen
buffets blow in from the east, pressure rising.

Pottery in the Cypress Hills

> "I'm going to say it now,
> are you listening? You can only get there
> by water."
>
> — Elizabeth Philips

Walking these prehistoric hills on tufted grass,
imagine the sea
of ice dragging rubble
across their ribs. The glacier's retreat
scratched out a belly made small by sky,
clouds absorbing the forgotten
footfalls of metatarsals.

In the wake of the melt,
a brace of broken bones, cracked
femurs weighted down with iron,
molars dug like an ache from the cheek of the hill,
and a layered cap of coal, hiding
the white mud your potter friends crave.
They excavate with wheelbarrows and shovels, sieving
out impurities without washing away the heart.

Clay pulses on the wheel, clay
moves between their fingers,
clay settles into the stillness of a tumbler,
the stain of iron oxide on its lips.

Kneel beside the potter, open
your palms, fill them with mud
as slippery as wet skin, cupping water
that spills from hands to wheel to soil. Close
your fingers on the clay, and feel life
taking shape again.

Acknowledgements

Thanks to my family and circle of friends for unshakable faith, generosity, kindness, and love. Thanks especially to Dave Margoshes, and to my wondrous big-sky editor, Barry Dempster. Thanks to my sons, Darl and Dailyn, to Rhekia Fahssi, and to Rosemary Griebel. Thanks to Phil Hall, Elizabeth Philips, Jeanette Lynes, Hilary Clark, Don McKay, Maureen Scott Harris, Karen Solie, Richard Harrison, Sue Goyette, Kelly Jo Burke, and Cathy Ostelere. Thanks also to my incredible Sage Hill friends, and to the Saskatchewan Writers' Guild Artists' and Writers' Colony staff and participants at St. Peter's Abbey and Emma Lake.

To my colleagues in Visible Ink and my double-cohort colleagues in the U of S's MFA in Writing program, thanks! Dim sum is on me.

To Paul Wilson, and the fine team at Hagios Press, thank you for the faith, and a special wowzer to artist Frances Werry for the stunning cover art.

Earlier versions of some of this work appeared in the following anthologies: *The Challenge of Three* (GritLIT, 2010), *None and All of This is True* (GritLIT, 2012), *Entanglements: New Ecopoetry* (Two Ravens Press, Scotland, 2012) and *Pith & Wry: Canadian Poetry* (Your Scrivener Press, 2010), and on CBC Radio's *Sound XChange*. Poems also appeared in *CV2*, *Prairie Fire*, *Room*, *Blue Skies*, *Other Voices*, *The Society*, *The Quint*, *The Antigonish Review*, *Event*, *Vallum*, *Grain*, *Freefall* and *The Fieldstone Review*. A selection from *wildness rushing in* won the 2012 Hamilton Poetry Festival's GritLIT poetry contest. Another multi-poem suite won third prize in the 2010 GritLIT contest, and was subsequently read on CBC Radio's *Sound XChange* by Kate Herriot. "Pottery in the Cypress Hills" was a shortlisted finalist in *The Malahat Review*'s 2010 Far Horizons Poetry Contest, and "Waiting for the loons" was a shortlisted finalist in *The Malahat Review*'s 2012 Far Horizons Poetry Contest. I thank small-press publishers, editors, and readers for keeping writers breathing in Canada.

I gratefully acknowledge the financial support of the Saskatchewan Arts Board, Access Copyright Foundation, and Sage Hill Writing, whose funding gave me the financial breathing space and time to write this book.

SHELLEY BANKS

dee Hobsbawn-Smith grew up in a gypsy Air Force family, much of her childhood spent in France, Cold Lake, Courtenay, Chicoutimi, and Chilliwack. dee returned to Saskatchewan in 2010 after a 34-year absence and lives in her family's old farmhouse west of Saskatoon with her partner, the poet and writer Dave Margoshes, and their dogs and cats. She is currently earning her Master of Fine Arts (M.F.A.) in writing at the University of Saskatchewan in Saskatoon with a creative thesis, a novel-in-progress titled *The Dryland Diaries*. In 2013, she was the first English Department graduate student to be awarded an Innovation and Opportunity scholarship granted by the U of S and the Saskatchewan government.

Her award-winning journalism, poetry, fiction, and essays have aired on the CBC and have appeared in books, newspapers, magazines, anthologies, and literary journals in Canada, the USA, and elsewhere, including *Grain*, *Gastronomica*, *Vallum*, *CV2*, *Prairie Fire*, *The Antigonish Review*, *The Malahat Review*, *The Windsor Review* and *Event*. She has written three best-selling cookbooks and her fifth book, *Foodshed: An Edible Alberta Alphabet* (Touch-Wood Editions, 2012), won the 2013 Gourmand World Cookbooks Awards "Best Food Literature" Award (Canada, English-language), and the Best Culinary Book Award at the High Plains Book Awards of 2013.

Wildness Rushing In is her first poetry collection. Her first collection of short fiction, *Appetites*, will be published in 2015 by Thistle-down Press.